CODE
OF ETHICS
FOR
SCULPTORS

followed by a
**PRACTICAL GUIDE TO THE RELATIONSHIPS
BETWEEN SCULPTORS AND CONSUMERS**

CONSEIL DE LA SCULPTURE DU QUÉBEC

WORK COMMITTEE
Jacques Besner, Ninon Gauthier, Denise Lapointe, Luc LaRochelle,
Jules Lasalle, Sylvie Rochette
RESEARCH AND WRITING COORDINATOR
Sylvie Rochette
PRODUCTION COORDINATOR
Louise Page
RESEARCH
Denise Lapointe
AUTHOR OF GUIDE AND APPENDICES
Ninon Gauthier
AUTHOR OF EXPLICATIVE NOTES PERTAINING TO COPYRIGHT
Me Luc LaRochelle
TRANSLATION
Liliane Busby
FRONT PAGE PHOTOGRAPH
Martin Brault
GRAPHICS AND PHOTOCOMPOSITION
Andrée Payette, The Reader's Digest Association (Canada) Ltd
PRINTING
Sponsor: Pratt & Whitney Canada

The CONSEIL DE LA SCULPTURE DU QUÉBEC is subsidized
by the Ministère des Affaires culturelles du Québec

CONSEIL DE LA SCULPTURE DU QUÉBEC

Dépôt Légal:
National Librairy of Québec
National Librairy of Canada
ISBN 2-920575-12-0

Printed in Canada

This publication has been made possible with the support of:
The Samuel & Saidye Bronfman Family Foundation
Ministère des Affaires culturelles du Québec
The Reader's Digest Association (Canada) Ltd
Pratt & Whitney Canada

Nota bene: throughout this work,the masculine form is used without
prejudice to the feminine and implies both female and male sculptors.

FOREWORD

This code of ethics is to be used as a guide and reference work as much by sculptors as by lovers of their works.

This work is published with various objectives in mind. The code of ethics intends making the identification of original works of art easier and also aims at protecting the sculpture market; it also wishes to better inform investors about the art field, increase their knowledge about sculpture as a profession and the works they acquire. The code of ethics establishes criteria that allow a difference to be made between the limited edition of a sculpture and its production with the help of industrial means. Apart from setting rules related to the practices that must be followed by every sculptor with regard to their relationships with each other and with the buyers of their works, this work also covers the techniques, materials, production and maintenance of sculptures. To this effect, we have also included a lexicon of terms specific to sculpture which should further the understanding of the practice of this profession.

You will also find information related to copyright, the use of contracts as well as the dispositions of the laws which affect the contractual relationships between a sculptor and his client and their intermediaries on the market. The relevant chapters found in the "Guide to the relationships between sculptors and consumers" aim at describing their mutual duties and obligations.

Finally, I wish to thank the members of the work committee for their precious collaboration, for this year spent in frequent meetings related to the writing of this work and for their interest with regard to the improvement of conditions in which sculptors execute their profession.

Louise Page
PRESIDENT, CONSEIL DE LA SCULPTURE DU QUÉBEC.

SYNOPSIS

Code of ethics for sculptors

The sculptor and his profession

1. The sculptor tries to achieve originality in his creative work.

2. The sculptor works in a climate of fair competition towards his peers, does not denigrate them to promote his own career, nor does he interfere with any transaction that is taking place between a colleague and a potential client.

3. In a context of invitations to tender, the sculptor conducts himself in an honest manner; he abstains from looking for information that is not available to his peers; if he does obtain such information, he behaves loyally, ascertaining that said information is made available to all participants.

4. The sculptor stands up for his profession and insures its promotion.

The sculptor in relation to buyers and users

1. The sculptor identifies his work by signing it with his name or pseudonym or still by affixing a distinctive mark on it. This mark is not necessarily noticeable on cursory examination.
—He thus asserts his paternity rights towards his work including all other intellectual ownership rights that ensue from it.
—By allowing the identification of his works, he facilitates the work of various contributors such as dealers, curators, restorers, critics and historians.
—However, in specific political contexts or in a context of

a production of works accessory to his main work to sustain livelihood, the sculptor reserves the right to remain anonymous. This is however an exceptional case.

—Otherwise, in an advertising context or for the diffusion of his work and if the case arises, the sculptor respects the buyer's wish to remain anonymous.

3. The sculptor undertakes a commissioned work only if he has the necessary competence to complete it or if he has access to it. If necessary, he gathers information and consults experts.

4. In the case of a collective work or one that necessitates collaboration during the conception phase of the work, the sculptor identifies his collaborators, that is, the co-authors.

Furthermore he allows the foundry or any other practitioner* to affix his **seal.**

However, he is free to identify or not the assistants and the workshop that helped with the technical execution of his work.

5. The sculptor clearly states his intention with regard to the degree of permanence of his work and specifies whether the aging process is included or not in its evolution.

He identifies the materials that were used and specifies in a realistic manner the type of maintenance suited to his work taking into account the characteristics of the materials used as well as their variable durability and the particular **environmental** conditions of the **installation** site.

In fact, for reasons of safety, evaluation or restoration, the user and buyer have the right to be informed about the materials that make up a **sculpture** unless the manufacturing process is a secret one.

The sculptor or his representative supplies the buyer with this information by using a technical specifications form that is in keeping with the form annexed to this code.

The sculptor keeps a copy of his technical specification forms or entrusts them to an agency for safekeeping.

6. At the start of **edition** or as soon as the sculpture is put up for sale, the sculptor determines the number that will make up the size of the edition and he scrupulously respects this intended number. After having designed and approved the **prototype,** the sculptor himself rigorously controls the number and quality of each **copy** and in

*Words written in bold face are defined in lexicon.

no case can he delegate this responsibility to a third party.

This means that only the works produced while the artist is alive and under his direct supervision have the right to be called **"original work of art"**. It follows from this that the edition of an original work of art is automatically interrupted when the artist dies whatever edition size was originally planned. The **posthumous works,** even if they are produced with the help of the prototype and with the help of the most competent craftsmen can under no circumstances be considered original works of art. At the very best, they constitute excellent reproductions and should be advertised and sold as such.

Each copy of an edition is numbered, the first number indicating the particular number attributed to this copy and the second number the total number of copies produced including the **artist's proofs** labelled AP (example:1/5). Is excluded from this number the **hors commerce** copy, a specimen that is used exclusively for advertising, promotion or information purposes.

Unless specified otherwise, all **moldings** are made from the same prototype and produced with the same material(s). This is also the case for **assemblings.** Any **heightening** or variation within an edition must be clearly described on the technical specifications form provided with the edition.

However, since it may take several years for an edition to be completed, the information pertaining to the variations within an edition apply only to the copies already produced.

All the copies that make up an edition must be perfectly true to the prototype from a formal point of view as well as from the point of view of technical perfection. In the case of an accident or technical defect which results in the slightest damage or modification of the quality or form the sculptor must prematurely interrupt the edition, giving greater importance to the upholding of quality and respect of the prototype.

7. Any work that, known to its author, is intended for public usage, must respect the safety of these users.

The accessibility to a work determines whether it is intended for public usage or not.

8. The sculptor must familiarize himself with any information he is given with regard to the possible **site** for his work and he takes into account the restrictions, physical or others, that are inherent in this site.

9. The sculptor honours his contractual committments and his verbal agreements with respect to the production, diffusion and marketing of his works; he also contends with the laws and regulations relevant to his work including safety standards, environmental protection legislations, the relevant construction regulations as well as the laws which regulate commercial activities.

10. When the sculptor participates in a **symposium** or similar event, he adheres to the spirit of the project he has presented and which has been accepted as such by the organizers.

He completes the work in the expected time limit in accordance with the work conditions offered and as previously proposed by the organizers.

Guide to the relationships between sculptors and consumers

The market of original sculpture

CHAPTER 1

Originality and multiplicity

In the same way as a limited edition engraving can be considered an original work of art as a painting or a drawing is considered as such, some sculptures that are produced in a limited number of copies can also be considered original works of art. This is frequently the case for **bronze** work because of the amount of time involved and the production costs for the prototype and **mold** which are very high and because of the nature itself of the processes and techniques involved. Each copy of the edition is then considered an original work of art. In this case the edition must be strictly limited

Originality of the work and control by the artist

We have seen that it is essential that the sculptor exerts a tight quality control over every phase of the production of his work for this work to be considered an original work of art. The artist must exercise this control over each **multiple** comprising the edition. This right to control or rather this responsibility is inalienable, whether by sale, gift or legacy. Only the artist can decide whether a copy of his work corresponds or not to his artistic project.

For the artist, this implies that he participates, at least through his presence and direction, if not manually, in every phase of production of the work he approves of by putting his signature on it. His signature is an attestation of authenticity and quality. This signature means that he is responsible for his work, that he is entirely accountable for its quality. In the case of a limited edition, the signature also guarantees the limit of the edition in question and the identity of every multiple in the same edition. The terms of the agreement with the foundry should insure that he retains complete control over his work and that the code of deontology of his profession is respected.

To make sure that no third party will eventually exploit his work and name or betray his reputation, the artist will either break his matrix or original mold once the edition is completed or mark it in such a way so as to prevent its use; he will also retain ownership of this prototype and provide specific instructions to limit its use for documentation purposes. To this effect, sculptors could use the guidelines proposed in the field of engraving. Furthermore, the artist should always keep his matrix, mold or prototype so that in the case of counterfeiting he can easily prove his paternity rights with regard to his work and therefore take legal action against the forgers and their accomplices.

While some countries such as the Federal Republic of Germany refuse to recognize any posthumous work as an original work of art, other countries, namely France, extend the right of control to eligible parties in the case of limited edition sculptures. Thus, the 1967 French legislation considers as "original works of art... the sculptures **cast** in a limited edition... and controlled by the artist or eligible parties".

However, the total edition must never exceed the prescribed number or that planned by the artist before his death. The heirs or eligible parties of Renoir, Rodin, Maillol and Germaine Richier have continued or still do reproduce in bronze the works of these artists until the maximum number of eight copies has been reached. The eligible parties of Suzor-Côté in Canada or those of Remington in the United States have even greatly exceeded these numbers.

In the United-States, a committee of the College Art Association in 1974 has looked at the question of limited edition sculpture. While it refused to completely condemn posthumous editions, this committee proposed some guidelines with regard to this practice, guidelines which, if respected, make it possible to tolerate posthumous editions. According to this committee, three main principles should preside over any intervention in this field. To begin with and before any other consideration, it is necessary to insure that the artist's intentions as well

10

as his personal standards of quality and ultimately his reputation be fully respected. It was deemed acceptable that an artist such as Rodin, Vasarely or Warhol tried to reach the greatest possible number of people and to directly respond to the demand for his work and that consequently, his works would be edited in greater numbers. It is the intention of the artist and his only which should prevail. Rules should allow for the consumer's protection, should insure his right to receive suitable informations and education related to the artistic value of works of art that are offered to him and his right to enjoy works of art of the greatest artistic quality. As a third factor only did the committee consider the protection of the legitimate interests of the heirs or eligible parties with regard to possible counterfeiters. The committee accepted posthumous editions when the artist had left sufficiently precise indications concerning his intentions regarding the methods and techniques to be used, the **alloys,** the **finish, patina** and **size of the edition.** This committee considered unacceptable any transposition of the work in a format or material other than that planned by the author since such transposition could endanger the artist's vision.

This extension of the right to control the work to eligible parties, generally his heirs, has given rise to several cases of misuse: poor quality of posthumous work, excessive number of multiples, overcastings, etc. The consumer has sometimes no reference point to distinguish between posthumous works and those works produced while the artist was alive; this does bring to much confusion about the market. The progress that has been made in casting techniques makes it more difficult to differentiate between the original copies and recent castings. This contributes to sustain a climate of insecurity and distrust that is detrimental to the market of **limited edition sculpture.**

Fetishism sometimes temporarily prevails over the logical aspects of the market. The most famous and distressing case illustrating this is that of the bronzes cast from Degas's waxes and plasters. Most of these copies are posthumous and have absolutely not been authorized by the artist who left no indications with regard to his waxes. During his lifetime, Degas authorized the **casting** of only three of his waxes and these in plaster, not in bronze. Nevertheless, the bronzes copied from his waxes or plasters, copies that can number up to 27 in the case of overcasting are much sought-after by misinformed art lovers. For instance, in a context of an euphoric market and that of a large "Degas" show, on May 10 1988 at Sotheby's in New York, a casting titled "Petite danseuse à quatorze ans" cast from a replica of the original wax and from which 27 copies were made was sold for the exorbitant price of 10,120,000 American dollars. This represents an absolute record for the sale of a sculpture in an auction, a fact that has been much commented upon and condemned by specialists.

Today's artists are more concerned about what will happen to their works after they die. Many now include in their will specific prescriptions which would justly prevent the proliferation of posthumous editions. Brancusi, while alive, refused to sign works whose production he had not completely controlled, and forbade through his will any posthumous editions of his prototypes. Henry Moore, also aware of the risk involved, destroyed his plaster prototypes for a long time. Finally, he decided on a compromise between his strict wish for absolute control of the production of his work and the scholars'need for information concerning his creative process. The plasters that had been used in the molding

Photo:
Casting studio before casting takes place. Containers which hold the models to be cast embedded in sand are visible on the floor. These models can be made from polystyrene which disappears during casting. The imprint left in the sand by the rigid mold can also be used as a mold. Photograph Martin Brault.

*(Professional Art Dealers Association of Canada)

of his bronzes would be in safekeeping in a museum where they could be studied but from which absolutely no casting could be made. The Art Gallery of Ontario was therefore entrusted with the greatest collection of drawings, sketches and prototypes by this artist as well as with some of his greatest works.

We cannot overemphasize the importance for contemporary sculptors to be guided by these examples. Still, it is necessary that the last wishes of the artist be fully respected. This is not always so. In the general framework of the adhesion of artists to this code of ethics it is to be hoped for that the last wishes of these artists be respected; these last wishes should prevail over the pecuniary interests of their heirs, eligible parties or museums.

In Canada PADAC*, a professional art dealers association makes exceptions for posthumous works that are controlled by eligible parties when these produce an edition that was previously authorized by the author and in whose production he was partially involved. However, this Canadian art dealers' association does not consider these posthumous copies as original works of art but as copies. In this, it is influenced by the definition itself of copyright, that is, literally meaning the right to copy.

In response to the needs of the consumer to protect himself and in an effort to improve the market of limited

edition sculptures, being inspired by the rules of ethics adopted by the members of PADAC and influenced by considerations relevant to the philosophy of copyright itself, we recommend that the control of an edition of a work be solely limited to the author of this work; therefore, no posthumous work could be designated under the name of "original work of art" and this even if the edition that was planned by the artist is not completed when he dies.

However, it still remains that some posthumous copies can be of excellent quality, that they may be scarce in number if the size of the edition strictly conforms to the wish of the artist and that they may increase tremendously in value in years to come. The copies produced by the Musée Rodin are of an excellent quality. They should still not be labelled "original work of art".

The question of authenticity:
dating, signature and workshop's seal
The fact that the artist's signature or his seal and the date are sometimes inscribed in the mold itself rather than subsequently etched onto the work, and the fact that the caster's seal is not always present contributes to the confusion seen in the market of limited edition sculpture and makes it more difficult to authenticate these limited edition original sculptures. How can one then know whether a work was produced while the artist was alive or not? The problems linked to authentification are much less important when the artist himself signs and numbers his work or when he and the caster both affix their seal on each copy rather than on the prototype.

This is why we believe that sculptors should sign, number and date each individual copy of their work and that the caster should also affix his seal. This practice provides the artist with a better control over his work and gives the consumer an additional warranty of authenticity. Furthermore, the caster's seal sometimes makes it possible to ascertain the date of casting when it is not included on the copy and also to know whether the work was produced while the artist was alive or not. When necessary, this practice may make the restoration of the work easier,since the caster is often the only person who knows the exact composition of the alloys and the acids used for creating a patina. However, it should be stated that the caster's seal does not confer on him any rights to the intellectual property titles attached to the work. This seal is a simple proof of the quality of the casting with regard to the technique and materials used. To avoid any

Photo:
Casting workers pouring the melted metal in the mold. Photograph by Martin Brault.

15

litigation, the sculptor would be well advised to include the copyright symbol in front of his signature. While this does protect more efficiently his copyright, it also facilitates his relationships with the future users of his work.

Still from the perspective of better informing the consumer, we propose that two dates be inscribed, that of the casting and that of the creation of the prototype. This last date would mainly be useful to specialists, art historians and museologists in the case of works that have been casted several years after the prototype was created, which is quite frequent for original **art bronze** works. The date of creation and that of casting should follow the fraction that expresses the number of the copy and the size of the edition, for instance[1/8, 1976-80].

The artist's hand

In France, apart from limited edition casts, the only works that are considered original works of art are,"...the productions using any material of statuary art, sculpture and assemblings... entirely executed by the artist's hand...". thereby excluded are all the works produced in workshops that are only partially executed by the artist's hand and this even if he entirely controls their production; are also excluded the works "... produced through mechanical, photomechanical or chemical means". This clause also excludes any creation or artistic production with the help of a computer or any other technological means.

This criterion seems to us to be much too restrictive, bringing art to the level of a trade or handicraft. It does not take into account past or contemporary artistic practices. From all times, sculptors have used assistants or other practitioners for executing their work. This practice was moreover much more widely spread during the Renaissance or during the XIXth century than it is presently, the artist's direct intervention and even his gestures being now quite prized. Few great masters of the past were entirely responsible for the production of their work. As a rule, the final work was an **enlargment** of a **maquette,** executed by apprentices and practitioners under the supervision and control of the author. This is how all of Henry Moore's **monumental** works were produced and these works are considered original works of art.

The XXth century artists who are aware of the opportunities of this era and which are fascinated by the progress of science and technology have frequently used industrial processes to produce their work. Motorized mobile sculptures, sculptures that include **holograms** or videos,

16

laser sculptures, computer-assisted works, environmental sculptures produced with the help of heavy machinery, or simple assemblings of found objects or elements produced in industry under the artist's supervision: all these are various forms of contemporary sculptures in which the sculptor intervenes more at the level of the mind rather than manually which are nonetheless considered fully original works of art. This is generally agreed upon by contemporary art specialists, artists, critics, art dealers and museum curators. To state that all the works that have not been entirely produced with the artist's hand are not original works of art would eliminate a great part of the art work produced during the XXth century.

We therefore adopt a wider definition which is more congruent with the artistic practices presently in use. Will be considered original works of art those unique or limited edition sculptures produced under the direct supervision of the artist during every phase of their production.

Limited edition of art and multiples

It is noteworthy that in several countries there exists a legislation distinguishing between original works and multiples. Only limited edition works, including the artist's proof are considered original works of art.

Originally, the artist proof's copies, labelled A.P. were intended for the artist's collection or those of his collaborators where they were supposed to remain during the lifetime of the artist. This explains why they have sometimes been confused with the hors commerce copies used only for documentation or advertising purposes. In fact, the artists' proofs labelled A.P. are frequently found on the market making it necessary to include them in the number which indicates the total size of the edition on the technical specifications form if not on the work itself (for instance AP I/IV/12, 1980). Any edition which exceeds the prescribed size should be considered an edition of multiples, the copies from this edition are then not labelled "original works of art".

The Bern and Paris convention ratified under the aegis of Unesco after the Second World War, limits the size of the edition of original sculptures: twelve for large sculptures and twenty-four for small format sculptures. The French government through its tax system, limits to eight the number of copies for these editions to be considered original works of art. To these copies can be added three to four artist proof or hors commerce copies necessarily labelled A.P. or H.C.. This rule holds whether these copies

17

were casted together or whether the casting was spread over several years which is frequently the case since casting is an expensive process. However, some degree of fiscal sufferance does exceptionally allow that the number of copies intended for sale reach twelve. In the United States, the Income and Taxation Department considers as original works of art only those works whose edition does not exceed eight copies. Obviously, the artist is free to exceed this statutory number if he so wishes.

French Law specifies an additional distinction: it differentiates between the numbered works of a generally small limited edition (generally less than a hundred copies) and those numbered works that are edited in often unlimited numbers. Often, the reproduction rights of these last sculptures that are neither numbered nor signed individually are sold at a lump cost to a caster, an art publisher, a silent partner by the artist or eligible parties in such a way that these have no control over the quality of the production of these works. These works should in no case be considered works of art; they are purely decorative objects. The value of these multiples can increase only in a limited fashion since the value of a work of art resides mainly in its quality, scarcity and is not only due to the reputation of its author.

As far as the buyer is concerned, this means that the price of a limited edition sculpture should reflect the character of the work involved, that is, allow a clear distinction to be made between the original work of art from a sculpture that has been numbered, either a limited edition or a multiple; the price should also be related to the size of the edition and this, whatever reputation the artist benefits from and in whatever demand his work is.In Canada, the appellation "limited edition original work" is not controlled as such. However, a few laws and regulations do provide some guidelines to this effect. Thus, the Canadian copyright law protects as works of art only those limited edition sculptures that do not exceed fifty in number. Intellectual property rights for larger editions must be registered by virtue of the Industrial Design Act. Revenue Canada is even stricter: sculptures that have an edition number that is greater than twelve are not considered original works of art and are thereby not exempted from the excise tax as far as imports are concerned, nor from the industrial tax for multiples of sculptures produced in Canada. This lack of coherence between the Canadian laws and regulations creates much confusion on the market. Since the number of international cultural and commercial exchanges is steadily increasing, we deem it necessary to propose the greatest strictness and clarity with regard to these questions and suggest that we be guided by the most stringent rules that are in effect in the countries with which we have cultural and commercial exchanges. We therefore recommend that the size of limited edition original works of art be restricted to twelve.

Obviously, castings or molded sculptures can also be unique works. They are then simply signed or what is most frequently done, numbered 1/1. In fact castings are generally edited in small numbers. This practice does provide a clear distinction between the unique work and the unlimited edition multiple which is often not even numbered.

All these considerations which are related to bronze works also apply to limited edition sculptures produced in other materials (aluminum, gold, silver, or other metals or alloys, glass, ceramics, acrylics, etc.). They also apply to the editions of works of art produced through assembling.

The rule of homogeneity with regard to the edition and the use of various patinas and materials
In the field of engraving, it is generally considered that all the copies of the edition of the same work must be absolutely identical.

This is not the case in sculpture. Even though the characteristics inherent to sculpture, its size, mass, volume, weight, surface texture must be respected, variations in color, finish, patina, coating and even texture are permissible. Frequently, several copies of the same sculpture can be found on the market, copies that were produced with different materials or showing a different patina or coating. Thus, the same sculpture can be cast either in aluminum, bronze or even in precious metals such as gold or silver. The finish can also vary a great deal, from green to blue, brown to black, from natural patina to applied patina, from brushed to polished, bronze and brass sometimes gleaming like gold or silver. These practices can be linked with those found in engraving where various **states** of the same etching can be produced or when an etching is heightened; these practices are also accepted in sculpture.

Even though we would prefer that, as far as the question of uniformity of edition is concerned, the same criteria that are used in engraving could be used in sculpture, we find it difficult to completely dismiss these

19

widely spread practices as does the College Council for the Arts. In its 1974 report, this American agency accepted as original works of art only those sculptures produced with the material that was planned for the final version by the artist. As far as we are concerned, we accept that a compromise be achieved between respect due to the consumer's rights and the wish of the artist as long as the consumer has been informed ahead of time of any change that occurs within an edition, whether these changes are planned at the beginning before the first copy hits the market or occur while the edition is being produced. In this last case, it seems to us that, from the simple point of view of respect due to the consumer's rights, the artist should ask for the authorization from the owners of the copies already sold before proceeding with any modification of material or finish of the work. This is particularly important when a change in material is envisioned and this change involves the use of a material that is less noble than that used for the first copies and therefore lesser in cost; the owners of these first copies could feel cheated.

As much as possible, the artist who wishes to use his right to modify the material or finish of a work that is being edited should warn the buyers by stating so on the identification form of the work and this, as soon as the first copy is sold.

It also occurs that sculptors increase the number of editions of the same work in relation with variations in materials and finish. This last practice runs counter to the deontological rules that we propose since it tends to give a false impression to the consumer concerning the actual size of the edition. At the very most, sculptors can, in this way,produce one or several editions of multiples in materials or finish other than those planned for the original version. Of course, these multiples will not be considered original works but reproductions. Finally, as in the previous case, the rule of strict consumer information must prevail before going ahead with such a project. In stating the size of the edition that is planned, the sculptor commits himself to respect this number.

Reduced and enlarged model
There is no law that precisely prevents the artist from carrying out **reductions** or enlargments of his work and various **scale** variations of the same sculpture model can frequently be found on the market. This is particularly true for the works of renowned or popular artists. How

20

should the sculptor behave? Can he indefinitely repeat the same form that appeals to art lovers by reducing or enlarging it of a tenth of a centimeter? What will then be the consumer's reference point surrounded by all these copies of various sizes? Should all these works be considered original works of art? If not, which edition, which scale should be preferred?

The section of French legislation that deals with original works refers to the artist's original project with regard to the final version of the work and considers that the copies of the series whose scale correspond to the initial wish of the artist should be considered original works of art. If, when the work was first designed, the artist chose to produce it in a small format, the enlargments of this work, except if important changes have been made, are considered to be copies. This holds true for reductions in scale, whether these are important or not.

American legislation shows more tolerance towards the reductions and enlargments that are directly controlled by the artist but still warns the artists against possible abuses of this practice. On the other hand, this legislation prohibits any posthumous reductions and enlargments even if these are controlled by the heirs or eligible parties unless the artist has left specific written prescriptions to this effect.

What if the artist first conceived his sculpture as a miniature? It is this size work which will remain the original format even if the artist later produces an enlargment of this same work. If he plans a monumental work, this work will then be recognized as the original work even if this work has first been created as one or several maquettes on a more or less small scale. For commissioned works, it may occur that the artist makes up several intermediate maquettes which help him evaluate the final result and if necessary bring about any corrective measures before the size and materials of the final version are used. The maquette is the equivalent in sculpture of the studies and sketches found in painting. It exists on its own which explains why it usually remains the artists' property.

In Canada, there is no legislation pertaining to the status of reductions and enlargments. The following criteria should therefore be taken into account in limiting the number of reductions and enlargments: common sense, the laws of the art market and the general rules which govern the consumer's protection; minimal variations in scale which could fool the consumer should be prohibited and furthermore these should be informed of the number of reductions and enlargments that are planned for a given model when the edition is placed on the market. If it so happened that the demand for his work prompts the artist to carry out reductions or enlargments that were not planned in the initial contract, he should to begin with obtain the permission to do so from all the owners of a copy of the work before proceeding with this project.

A **gallery owner** has suggested to us that these variations in scale: small table-size, average size and a very large format, this last generally intended for outdoors. He also proposed that the number of the average-size edition should not exceed three while monumental works should not be copied. He stated that this is the practice currently in use and even the rule in some European countries. We have failed to find any confirmation of these practices or legislations in the various reports we have consulted.

We are not proposing that such strict limits should be accepted but we do strongly urge sculptors to be both honest and careful in their dealings. The art market is a particularly fragile one: the smallest uncertainty may well destroy it. It is therefore imperative that consumers be respected by supplying them with the correct information about the size of the edition and the number of variations in scale of the work that is offered to them. Both artist and art dealers should remember that rarity plays a major role in price assessment and appreciation of works of art. Flooding the market in response to a specific demand may well result in the destruction of this same market on a mid to long term basis. The difference in price between those works whose scale correspond to that of the final version planned by the artist and those varying-scale works, enlargments and/or reductions should clearly allow a distinction to be made between the format of the final version and those other formats. The size of the editions of these various scales works could also provide the consumer with precious guidelines. Thus, a greater number of reductions or enlargments could be produced even possibly an unlimited number that could be sold at a relatively low price which would prevent any confusion.

Art lovers should be extremely vigilant and well informed about the works of art they wish to purchase as they are about any other product they acquire. In the case of important acquisitions, they should get informations from

Photo:
Casting itself. Smoke and flames escaping from the mold after casting can be seen at the center of the photograph. Photograph by Martin Brault.

art books and magazines, catalogs of shows, reasoned catalogs; they should also not hesitate to look for advice from experts which have information about the coveted work, its authenticity, originality, size of edition. We suggest that these elementary rules of caution should always be respected, particularly in a country such as Canada where the market of the limited edition sculpture has not yet been regulated.

The works of renowned or popular artists are particularly susceptible to the occurrence of frauds, **overmolding** or other counterfeiting practices since, generally, demand exceeds the supply offered. This is where it is most probable to find editions in excessive numbers and almost unlimited reductions and enlargments. The case of the popular American sculptor Frederic Remington and that of Auguste Rodin are well known. These artists' works have been subjected to numerous overmoldings, reductions, enlargments and very high number editions even while these artists were alive. One must however remember that there was then no strict regulations concerning art bronzes. Some artists of the past and present have opted for profit sometimes sacrifying quality to quantity.

In its 1974 report, the 1974 College Art Association of the United-States recommended that all posthumous copies and reproductions of a sculpture be clearly identified as such when they are marketed. They added that such information should be clearly inscribed on the object itself or on its identification plate. Furthermore, this data should be included on all invoices related to the successive sales of this work, in the advertising material or in the show catalogs or other publications where the work is mentioned or shown. They also stated that the responsibility for providing adequate information should rest equally on the artists and their eligible parties and on the other concerned parties: art dealers, auctioneers, museum curators or art critics. We entirely agree with these recommendations.

Technical specifications forms*

The problems that are found in the market of original limited edition sculpture are largely dependent on the lack of information of consumers and the absence of regulations on the labelling of works of art. We therefore propose that artists, collectors, art dealers use a technical specifications forms on which could be found precise information about the sculptures offered for sale.

Artists, gallery owners and artists'agents can also

Photo:
Reduction model of the monumental sculpture "Le malheureux magnifique" by Pierryves Angers, 1972. At the center (white part) is found the definitive Hydrocal model which was used to make the flexible rubber mold used for the edition of the plaster, plastic or wax sculpture. On the outside (pale grey portion) the investment can be seen, a rigid material used for holding the flexible rubber mold during casting. The wax model was used for metal casting this multiple in the foundry. Photograph by Robert Etcheverry.

*An example of a technical specifications form and maintenance estimate sheet can be found in the appendix.

25

receive, free of charge from the Conseil de la sculpture du Québec the form which deals with the technical restoration estimate of works of art, form devised by the Centre de conservation du Québec. This form attempts to promote the cooperation that is essential between the artist and the restorer.

When these works are resold, this technical information sheet should be given to the new owner of the work along with the maintenance specifications sheet. Apart from guaranteeing the authenticity of the work and the limits of the edition which would protect the consumer against frauds, this form would facilitate insuring the work and eventually its resale. The historicity of the work could also be made easier if a list of all successive owners of the work was annexed; resale will also then be less difficult. We all know that for works of similar quality, those that are well documented.are often sold at better prices. On a mid-term basis, the existence and use of such an identification form could help clear up this market and establish a climate of trust at least as far as contemporary art is concerned.

It would be useful to append to this form one or several photographs of the work authenticated by the artist which could be used for identifying and insuring the work as well as restoring it if this becomes necessary. The form stating the specifications for maintenance that would also be included would prevent the consumer from causing irreparable damages to the work and would also allow the restoration of the work to be faithful to the artists's intentions.

Conservation and restoration of sculptures

Attitudes towards the permanence and **conservation** of works of art has much evolved during the XXth century. In the past, it was thought necessary to preserve the final aspect of a work of art at any cost; the work of art being then considered a symbol of the triumph of mind over matter, it should be timeless and should not be subject to the ravages of time. Today, time has become a factor that is most often taken into account, the natural evolution of matter being accepted by both artists and lovers of their work.

The conditions under which works of art are conserved have changed a great deal. Of course, today, we are more aware of the ideal methods for conserving the various materials from which the works are built and we should therefore be better equipped to prevent the effects of

26

time. However, the increase in pollution makes this control rather uncertain. Public works and works that are situated outdoors are particularly vulnerable and we must now even question the permanence of marble and patined bronze, materials which had the reputation of being almost totally resistant to the effects of time. Pollution sometimes affect them irremediably as it affects all other material objects. At the present time, artists cannot completely guarantee the perennity of their work. At the very most, the sculptor can reassure the consumer that he has taken all necessary measures in choosing the tested materials, that these were selected with regard to the site that is planned, the techniques and methods used and that he has provided him with the relevant informations concerning the components of the work as well as its use and maintenance.

Art lovers should also ask about the probable permanence of a work and the maintenance of a sculpture before buying it; they should also find out if it was designed for indoors or outdoors. If they have no such information, they should enquire from the artist or another expert before placing a sculpture outside or before proceeding with the maintenance or cleaning of one of their collection pieces. Some cleaning agents, some waxes or some varnishes could irremediably damage the patina or finish of a sculpture thereby reducing its sale value. The author of the work, the conservation departments of museums or the Centre de conservation du Québec could supply such information to those who request it. The collector should never attempt to restore a sculpture that has been damaged. No matter the fees asked by a restoration expert, it would still be more economical to hire him rather than commit an irreparable mistake which would irremediably result in the devaluation of the work. Large museums, the Centre de conservation du Québec in Québec or the Canadian Association of Professional Restorers can supply the name of experts in your area.

On the other hand, the curiosity and taste of modern and contemporary artists for innovation and research has often led them to use new materials whose resistance to pollution and weather had not yet been tested or materials whose characteristics had been overestimated by the manufacturer. Thus, synthetic materials such as Corten steel or Stelcoloy which had been developed to increase the resistance of steel to humidity and which have been widely used by artists in the sixties have proven to be more sentitive to pollution and less reliable than had been predicted by the manufacturer. Today, several artists who used these materials now have to treat them to stop **corrosion.** They have to modify the way the surface was initially supposed to look, that is, velvety red. Each sculptor chooses a solution which best corresponds to his vision of the work. Thus, in the United States, Tony Rosenthal has decided to paint over in black most of the sculptures that he produced with these materials, therefore emphasizing the form of the work rather than the color or texture. Charles Ginnever has preferred keeping the natural aspect of the metal and recommends that his raw steel sculptures be periodically brushed and oiled. This type of intervention should be solely decided by the artist as he is the only one who can decide whether the finish of the work can be modified and how this can be done. As much as possible, he should state what he intends with regard to the evolution of his work at the time of sale or even at the time of creation.

The use of organic materials is particularly risky from the point of view of conservation since their degradation occurs more readily than that of inorganic materials and since it is particularly difficult to arrest, even slow down, the process of degradation once it has begun.

Moreover, the parasites that these materials may harbour, could possibly contaminate the surrounding works of art, works that are sometimes of great value. The artist who, through his work, introduces parasites in a collection of works could be prosecuted for doing so. On the other hand, some materials when used alone can be conserved but if used in combination with others are found to be incompatible, which also contributes to the degradation of the objects they are made of. It is therefore important that sculptors be very careful in using new materials, or waste materials as well as when assembling various materials. If they decide to use waste materials, they should decontaminate them before including them in their works. They should also have adequate information about the resistance of materials they intend using, the conditions in which they can be used and should warn the potential buyers of the possible risks incurred when they use materials that have not been completely tested. On the other hand, sculptors should not be blamed if they have themselves been misinformed or cheated by the manufacturers of a new material. The buyers should themselves be aware of these risks and assume these jointly with the artist when, in all good faith they choose a work that was produced with new materials or with the help of new techniques.

It may happen that the artist plans these transformations of the work through the effects of climate, the resulting patina, its aging or even the public intervention through graffitis; the artist may consider that these are normal and he may even wish for these to occur. If this is in fact his wish, he should warn the buyer at the time of sale or commission. The owner will then have to respect this vision of the artist, the restoration of the work then being always dependent on this vision.

Because of specific production methods or materials, some sculptures are intended for indoor use only. Some can only be moved using extensive precautions. The artist should so inform the buyer who in turn must respect these dictates. When the artist adequately informs the buyer with regard to the limits of utilization of his work, this buyer can then hold the artist responsible for a premature deterioration of the work only if he has rigorously followed the prescribed indications. On the other hand, when the collector buys a work of art, he accepts some responsibility concerning the work which, in a way, becomes part of our cultural heritage; from this stems the moral obligation to respect the prescribed usage of the work.

Several contemporary artists try to express their apprehension towards the future by using specific techniques and materials. In all conscientiousness, they choose to use perishable materials and techniques or manufacturing processes which result in particularly fragile works and even in self-destroying works. This process of destruction, planned by the artist is an integral part of the work. The creators of these works must absolutely warn the collector of these facts who then knowingly accepts or not the ephemeral character of his esthetic pleasure and the impossibility to consider his acquisition an investment.

This information about the potential and conditions of conservation of the work should be included in the maintenance fact sheet that is attached to the technical specification form and handed over to the buyer and a copy placed in archives. It is to be understood that these responsabilities for informing the consumer should also be accepted by the intermediaries which represent the artist in dealings with clients.

The sculptor and commercial practices

The sculptor is a professional who like other artists attempts to earn a living through his work. His production costs are however much higher than those of **engravers,** draft artists or painters. The materials he uses are generally much more expensive. The type of materials that are used, the complexity of the techniques and processes used in sculpture, the strength required, all of these factors often force him to ask for help from assistants, practitioners or technicians, even engineers, all of whom must be remunerated. His tools are also often more numerous and sophisticated and their cost is sometimes quite high.

The risks he incurs in his work increase his insurance costs. The tridimensional character of his work as well as their weight require the use of a larger studio and adds to his costs for storage and transportation. Since the sculptor wishes to earn a living through his work, he cannot ignore his production costs when pricing his works. This explains why even though the sculptor generally benefits from a smaller profit margin, he still has to ask for a much higher price than that normally asked for a similar size work produced by these other artists. If he lowers his prices below that of his production costs, he transgresses the rules of fair competition that are set by his code of ethics.

As is true for any other manufacturer, the sculptor must honor his contractual committments and his verbal agreements with respect to the realization, diffusion and marketing of his works. The responsibilities of the artist also include respecting the planned size of the edition, quality standards, legislations touching upon the environment and supplying the consumer with correct information regarding his work.

On a wider basis, the artist must also respect all laws, rules and regulations which control commercial practices. The Québec law on the status of the artist provides a framework for these practices and sets up rules of conduct for the artist and their commercial partners. Thus, this law supplies minimal foundations on which can rest the contractual relationships between artists and their partners. Furthermore, as is true for any other field, any business relationship between the artist and his partner should be based on a contract regulating these relationships. As far as collective works are concerned or still when work requires the collaboration of practitioners or other technicians, a contract should be used which clear-

Photo:
Jordi Bonet, "Exemplaire unique, série des oiseaux # 7321", aluminum cast, 1/1, (11"X24"X5"), 1973, Reader's Digest Collection. Aluminum sculpture directly cast from a polystyrene prototype which disappears during casting. Photograph Martin Brault. Courtesy of Reader's Digest Association (Canada) Ltd.

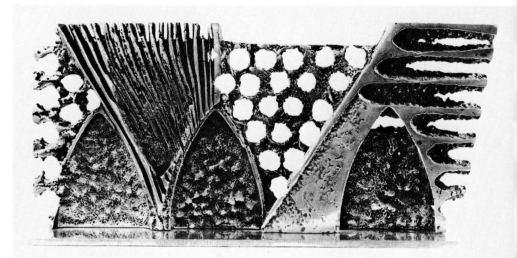

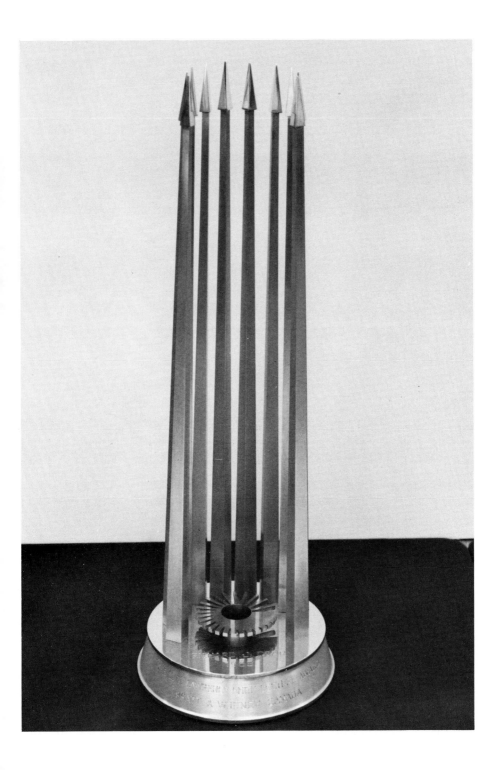

ly stipulates to whom belong the propriety rights or in what way they should be shared. To avoid any litigation, this contract should also entrust the management of the intellectual property rights to one of the collaborators.

Among these rules of conduct, loyalty towards his commercial partners, co-authors, agents or dealers is of prime importance. Thus, the artist must respect the normal pricing he has established with his intermediaries and should stick to one price on the market; if he fails to do so he may well create a climate of insecurity and instability, climate which is harmful on a long term basis and may well cost him precious allies. In the same manner, he must adhere to the agreements he has reached with his representative(s), refusing to directly intervene in any transaction or even relationship that has been initiated by one of these representatives. If he sells work directly in his studio, he must follow the fiscal laws and collect the sales tax.

This implies that in his commercial dealings with the artist, the consumer must accept the artist's obligations towards a third party. Any attempt by the consumer to influence the artist to derogate from his obligations and agreements may threaten the stability of the market and on a long term basis may affect the value of the work thus acquired. It is essential that the rules of the game must be followed by all commercial partners so that the sculpture market may be a healthy one.

Art lovers have the right to privacy and it may happen for various reasons, including the possibility of theft, that they may request from the dealer or artist that they remain anonymous and that their ownership of a work of art not be publicly disclosed. Before divulging in a curriculum vitae or any other publication or still to a third party, the name of a private collector, the artist and his dealer must obtain the authorization from the collector.

Commissioned works of art

Commissioned works of art and autonomy of the artist

We have seen in the previous chapter that modern and contemporary artists claim absolute control rights over their work and on the definition of its finality. At first glance, this attitude seems to contradict the nature of a commissioned work itself where the finality of the work, its environment, as well as some of its most important characteristics such as the dimension, theme, subject

Photo:
The sculptor Louis Archambault has created this work for the Pratt & Whitney Canada in 1989. This sculpture is awarded every year to a scientist giving a talk to the Elvie Lawrence Smith Lecture Series; this sculpture was designed and produced by the artist with the help of computers at the Pratt & Whitney Canada in Longueuil. Photograph Sydney Jones. Courtesy of Pratt & Whitney Canada.

33

matter, the materials used are defined not by the author but by the client. Furthermore, in the context of a democratic society like ours, the public, represented by the users, also intervenes with respect to the finality of the work, some of its main characteristics and its esthetic value. Under these conditions, how can there be room for the artist's freedom, a freedom that is deemed essential to the quality of his expression? Yet, in the XXth century, commissioned public work of arts have increased in number. In this chapter we will see how it is possible to harmonize these varying viewpoints and these contradictory objectives within the framework of various types of commissions.

Public art and private art
It is first of all important to distinguish between private art and **public art** both of which can be owned privately or publicly. Private art is essentially aimed at the owner's pleasure and also that of his immediate circle and/or his employees. Only exceptionally does the public have access to it, that is, when he is admitted within the owner's world. The relationship which then occurs between the onlooker and the work is a free and intimate relationship. Most of the **art objects** found in the collections of private individuals or firms belong to the private domain, no matter what size the works are. Even though they belong to the public domain through their owner, works that are found in public collections or museum collections are not public works of art per se, independently of their size. In fact, except for some cases, the public has no access to these works unless he decides to go look at them.

Public art, whether privately or publicly owned, is accessible to the public at all times. Whether the work is inside or outside a building, the public work of art is inescapable and this even more so since its dimensions are often monumental. Because of its location, this works always stands out; its size may also increase this effect. A sculpture that is located in a square, a park, a garden or still in the hall of a public building or a building inhabited by tenants becomes because of this, a public work of art.

A sculpture placed in front of the head office of a firm or in the front garden of a private individual could also be considered public art. This last position is that adopted by the City of Montréal Public Art Program.

Since public art is exceptionally visible, this largely contributes to the education of the public at large. This public work is then also particularly vulnerable to verbal and physical attacks from this same public. At the end of the sixties, a mobile sculpture made by Jean Gauguet-Larouche was chained up on the Alma public square since it had been judged too noisy. In New York, the rusted surface of a Cor-ten sculpture by Richard Serra roused much anger from the employees working in an adjacent building, so much so that they asked for it to be removed. Moreover, it is rare to find in this great art metropolis, sculptures that have not been the target of graffiti artists. Nevertheless, the permanent presence of an avant-garde sculpture may eventually modify people's views of such art. The Eiffel Tower which created quite a scandal a century ago is now for the Parisians, one of their favorite **monuments.**

Monumental works and others

What separates the commissioned work from the other works of a sculptor is that it arises as a direct response to a precise request from a client. It is the client who is to begin with at the origin of the work. This of course does not preclude that this demand also satisfies the needs for expression of the artist and that finally this demand becomes subservient to this need. This correspondence between the expectations of the client who has selected the artist on the basis of past works and the need for expression of the artist is eminently desirable for the work to really be successful. Furthermore, the client should leave enough scope to the artist in defining the project so that the work may exceed the demand, and reflect the artist's vision.

The words "commissioned work of art" generally suggest the idea of monumental work. However, small and average size works can also be commissioned whether they are to be exhibited indoors or outdoors. Portraits, either a **bust** or **statue** are often and have for a very long time been commissioned works. This is also true for other commemorative objects such as medals, statuettes, trophies which are offered to remember an anniversary, emphasize an important event, honour a person of mark or thank a collaborator. These gifts are not the prerogative of governments or large corporations. Firms and even private individuals can also commission and offer this type of art work.

Sculptures can also be commissioned for purely decorative purposes. Esthetics can then be combined with usefulness. In this way, an art lover could commission a

35

sculpted frieze, a fountain, a piece of furniture: table, console or chair, an architectural element which while maintaining its usefulness would stand out because of its esthetic and poetic qualities. Both esthetic and functional requirements will then have to be taken into account.

Very few sculptors would produce such work on their own. These are generally produced in response to commissions by collectors, designers, gallery owners or for thematic exhibits. It is also possible to commission a work to complete one's collection. The commission is then linked to the client's need for participation in the definition and control of the work.

Because of their size, production costs and storage difficulties, monumental works are usually commissioned. In the context of a major exhibit, the artist may produce such work on his own and defray the cost to satisfy his need for expression; this work would then rarely be the final version of the work. Most frequently, he will present a prototype produced in a less costly material than that planned for the final version. If this final version is eventually commissioned, the work will then be produced with this material and simply inserted on the site for which it was destined. The client's intervention is then minimal, generally extending only to the selection of the work. He may however sometimes also participate in the choice of the site, the lighting system and sometimes the pedestal. The nature and finality of the work are still mainly defined by the artist.

Sculpture and integration
Particularly if they are public or para-public organizations, the clients may look for a greater cohesion between the public work of art and the site where it will be found. The artist then designs his sculpture in relation to its future location and its physical, social and esthetic characteristics; the function of the location and general traffic will also be taken into account. Thus, the client must then define more closely the commissioned work thereby limiting even more the artist's freedom. One then talks of integration of the work of art to its environment.

This **integration** can be made a posteriori, once the building is already completed. It is generally advisable to associate the artist to the architect and other specialists involved in the construction at the start of the project. This allows for easier interactions and a more successful integration.

The artist may sometimes collaborate with the architect to the esthetic design of the building or of that section of the building where the work of art will be inserted. At the limit, the work of art could become an integral part of the architecture or furniture of the building, **reliefs** will be transformed into grids, portals, stairs, mantelpieces, benches, luminaries, wall coverings for elevators, a garden. Art then becomes akin to design.

The environment is a basic principle of integrated sculptures. In creating this work, the artist must take into account the physical characteristics of the future site, this site being either a natural one such as a park or one that has been created. The artist may even be called upon to consider all the aspects of the site. For instance, for the creation of a sculpture-fountain that will be placed in a garden close to a building or even for a sculpture that will be situated close to windows largely open to the countryside, the artist may be asked to take into account both the architecture and the exterior natural environment.

While elaborating his project and choosing the site of his sculpture, the artist must also consider the frequentation of the site, the busy circuits used by people and even their age or other characteristics. Safety standards could prevent a sculpture from being installed close to highly frequented circuits. On the other hand, a sculpture that is activated by a photomechanic cell will have to be placed close to such an area so that the users may regularly activate its mechanism. If this is not done, this sculpture would lose much of its interest and may even break down from disuse.

It may occur that an even greater integration of the work to the site may be desired. What is then aimed at is a sort of symbiosis with the socio-cultural milieu to which it is destined, hoping thereby to make the work more acceptable to the users. For instance, the artist will be asked to take into account the function of the building involved when designing his work. In this perspective, a definite subject or theme could assist the artist's creation. This approach has sometimes been used for some projects within the Québécois program for integration of works of art to the environment; this has particularly been the case for the integration of art works to centers for aged persons or for schools. Thus, a grid for a primary school built by Armand Vaillancourt was strongly influenced by children's drawings.

The integration of sculpture to specific sites restricts the artist to working in a particular manner, at the limit, the integrated work becomes indissociable from the context for which it was created. Its future is almost irremediably linked to that of the site. From this stems the major moral responsibility incurred by the owner of an integrated work of art to respect the right of the artist to protect the integrity of his work.

Advantages and disadvantages of integration

There are obvious advantages to the integration of art works. From an esthetic point of view, the final result may well be more balanced, more harmonious. This last objective can best be attained if the artist is involved when the architectural project is first initiated. More importantly, it is essential that the architect and artist respect each other. A real collaboration, even a complicity should take place between them.

When this collaboration does occur, the final quality of the integration and its artistic and architectural elements could contribute to increasing the sales value of the building or that of the site. The impact of a work of art on the gain in value of a building will be proportional to the fame or renown of the artist involved at the time of construction or later on.

Finally, if the socio-cultural context in which the sculpture will stand is taken into account, the users may find it easier to accept it resulting in less resistance and vandalism. However, this last precaution is often not sufficient to have the public art work valued and appreciated by a milieu that has not been adequately prepared to do so. These precautions cannot replace the communication and artistic training that are tools essential to the integration of public art works in the milieu they are designed for.

But there are also disadvantages to the integration of art work. To begin with, integration does limit the artist's freedom. It may curb his creativity, the vivacity of his expression, even bring about a depersonalization and standardization of the works produced in this context. When one tries too hard to please, to melt into the environment, to aim for neutrality, the resultant sculpture may well lose its rigour and artistic value. The work of art affects us, moves and disturbs us either pleasantly or unpleasantly. Restriction that are too important can affect its esthetic quality which will inevitably have a negative effect on its future sales.

On a long term basis, the presence of an integrated work can be problematic if the building is being renovated or alienated. Since the site is an integral part of the work, it cannot be modified without also modifying the

38

work itself. A major change in the site or moving the art work itself modifies the sculpture involved. These modifications cannot be made without the express authorization of the artist who has the moral right recognized by law to protect the integrity of his work. Before moving a sculpture when a building is being transformed or torn down, it is necesary to obtain the artist's authorization and agree with him about the methods involved. This may result in major additional costs especially if the work is so well integrated to the architectural elements that it seems indissociable from it. These conditions may even make more difficult the resale of the building.

In summary, before determining the nature of the commission it is important to clearly delineate the pros and cons of an integration and to specifically state in the contracts the respective responsabilities, the limits of their interventions and to plan for the eventuality of an alienation or moving of the work. Finally within this contract, it should be clear that the artist has sufficient freedom to create a personal work.

Stages in commissioning a work of art and method of selection

Once the nature and specific needs of the commission have been clarified, the artist who will produce it must be selected. If the client is a private individual or the head of a firm, he may well choose directly an artist whose work he knows and admires.

The client may sometimes widen his range of choices. Interesting sources of information are the following: art publications, books and magazines, data banks from artists's associations such as le Conseil de la sculpture du Québec and Visual Art Ontario, slide libraries of museums, universities, governmental agencies such as the Direction du programme d'intégration d'oeuvres d'art a l'environnement du gouvernement du Québec or the Art work bank of the National Council for the Arts of Canada. These services are generally free.

The client may sometimes be advised by a designer, an architect, a gallery owner, an artist's agent or still by an independent expert who, taking into account the client's tastes, need and budget, will suggest a few names or dossiers of artists from which the client will make his choice. This solution will be used if the budget of the commission is a relatively important one. It is generally much wiser to remunerate one's advisers. In this way one makes sure of their rigour and professionalism. The consultant's fee should be much lower than that of the total cost of the commission. One should get the relevant information with regard to the current fees allowed members of jurys or advisers from artists's association or governmental agencies who frequently request such services.

If the client is a large firm, a public corporation or agency and the budget that is granted is important enough, it may be interesting, even necessary, to assemble a jury and proceed using the competition formula.

This jury will be made up of experts and some of the client's representatives, usually executives or employees that have some knowledge about art or at least show some interest for it. The participation of these representatives in the process of selection will insure that the objectives of the firm will be taken into account when the jury deliberates; it will also provide moral guarantee for the selected artist and will facilitate the **insertion** of the work in the daily life of the agency or firm. If the client is a public agency that supplies services, one of the users of these services could also be a member of the jury; of course, this person must be representative of the milieu.

The experts will be chosen because of their competence, their knowledge of sculpture and the artistic milieu involved. As much as possible, one should diversify the jury, its origin, training, orientation so that the greatest possible number of choices is made possible. If the client is a firm, the selection of the jury could also be influenced by personal affinities this last being absolutely unacceptable if the client is a government agency, at least in a democratic society.

Each method of selection has advantages. The selection using only one step, with or without a jury is more economical and faster. It is also more relevant to small projects. Selection through a competition is a process that is relatively long and costly and is more frequently used for large projects.

Whether the artist is selected through an existing data bank or through a competition the selection process itself could be carried out in a single step or in several. If a single step selection is adopted, it is prudent to plan for one or several substitutes in case the selected candidate refuses the work or desists himself. In this last case, the client, helped or not by a jury, will choose a few artists whom he will ask to present a sketch or maquette designed to fulfill his needs. The client will then have to plan for a fee to be given to all the artists that are asked to participate in the competition, fee which should be propor-

Photo:
Tatiana Démidoff-Séguin working on the texture of her relief integrated in the hall of the Horizon School in Le Gardeur; this work is constructed with concrete- "ciment-fondu" and oxyde. A false perspective has been hollowed out at the bottom of the relief and echoes the long corridor which opens into the hall and emphasizes the idea of passage thereby contributing to the integration of the sculpture to the surrounding architecture.

tional to the importance of the work requested and the importance of the commission. Thus, the artists should receive a few hundred dollars for a sketch but if a maquette with plans, sketches and estimate is requested this fee could reach up to 5 000$ for each participant.

The complexity of the selection process, the numbers of jury members and the number of artists pre-selected should be directly related to the size of the project and the importance of the budget. Thus it will be useless to proceed with a public competition and ask several artists to present a maquette for a project dealing with a trophy with a budget of a few hundred or thousand dollars. On the other hand, it may be very interesting, if a budget of a few tens of thousand dollars is available, to use such a public competition: apart from increasing the range of choices and limiting the selection to artists that are truly interested, this approach may result in important advertising benefits. This may be particularly interesting for a firm that wishes to enhance or modify its image. A public competition is mandatory in the case of government agencies.

As soon as the competition is launched, the client must provide the artist with the main information concerning the nature of the project, the possible restrictions, the budget, the time limit, etc. If one is looking for a stone sculpture, it is useless to call for all sculptors. It will then be advisable to deal with those artists having the required knowledge. For some major projects requiring specific expertises, the client may wish that the artist work with other expert technicians, practitioners, architects or engineers. The client may also wish to evaluate the competence of these experts and that of the artist. Furthermore, he may also require some information regarding the artist's collaborators at the time of selection.

If the budget is only 10 000$ for a large format sculpture, it is essential that the artists that are invited to submit their candidacy be so informed. This will prevent some sculptors whose prices greatly exceed this amount from doing useless work and will encourage the participants to be more realistic towards this project. The client's expectations and the work conditions must also be made clear when the competition is launched or the invitation made.

The client will then have to give the same information to all the candidates to avoid the situation where one artist benefits from additional insights which could embarrass him with respect to his colleagues and his code of deontology.

Photo:
Building site. Installation of "Embâcle" at the Place du Québec in Paris; this fountain-sculpture by Charles Daudelin is an integration work awarded through a competition set up by the Québec Government. The flagstones made up of Muntz metal are imbedded in the pink Tarn granite paving of the Place; this paving, also designed by the artist, fits into the paving network of the surrounding streets. Photograph by the artist.

43

If such a situation became known, the client's reputation could be blemished thereby limiting the advertising benefits of the commission. In the same way, the client or jury who assesses the candidacy in a competition should only look at the documents that were requested. For instance, if one of the candidates has presented a maquette even though only a sketch was asked for, the client should ignore the proposed model and use only those requested documents to evaluate the candidate.

From the maquette to the work itself
The maquette provides several advantages. It allows the artist to confirm his interest for the project defined by the client, to evaluate his capacity to fulfill the client's expectation taking into account the restrictions involved, to formulate anew his vision with regard to these restrictions and to concretize his artistic project.

For the client, the maquette gives precise information with regard to the artistic solutions provided by the sculptor and makes it possible for him to visualize the project in the site for which it is planned.

However, the maquette constitutes only the first step of the creation of a monumental work. It is neither a mold nor model which is closer to the final version. While producing this maquette, the artist will probably have to readjust his project in response to the modifications in scale and materials, to the impact of the environment on his work and to his own evolution.

The client must not expect that the final version will simply be an enlargment of the scale model. There is always a discrepancy between the maquette and the final version of a large sculpture.

This difference between the maquette and the final version is the reason why, contrary to molds and models, the maquette always belongs to the artist and not to the client and this even if the artist is remunerated for it. In fact, this remuneration is simply an allowance for the research and creation involved in the artist's project and not for the art work produced during this research. If the client wants to own the maquette, he must negotiate this within the framework of the contract dealing with the maquette or that contract dealing with the commission, the price then being related to the artist's usual prices and not to the budget of the project. Some artists produce limited editions of these maquettes of monumental works which are put up for sale. This is a legitimate practice in so far as the backer or owner of the monumental

44

work is previously informed of the artist's intention or of the existence of such an edition if it has been produced before the monumental work was created and if he authorizes such an edition. It would be advisable to include a relevant clause in the contract. This edition should then be considered to be a reduction.

It is generally necessary to set up publicity support inside and outside the agency involved with the project, whether this is a private or public one. The client should make sure that he will be able to exhibit and reproduce the maquette, estimate, sketches, the photographic elements as well as the biography of the author, in other words, all the documents related to the commission which could facilitate the insertion of the work in the social milieu to which it is prioritarily destined.

Usually, the client is authorized to reproduce the scale model and sketches only for the time period necessary for the work to be completed.

In some cases, for instance, when public or para-public agencies are concerned, this authorization can extend up to five years after the commission contract has been signed. The reproduction rights of the final version should be negotiated within the commission contract. They could be bought for a lump sum or still be negotiated according to the precise needs of the client. Each individual case must be looked at separately and take into account the requests and particular needs of both the client and the artist.

Contracts dealing with the commission of works of art*
The idea of a commission appeals to you. Whether you are an artist, collector, head of a firm or an elected representative, you will have to negotiate an appropriate contract. A good contract is one that protects the client's interests while respecting the rights and freedom of the artist. It should not be excessively complicated while still trying to prevent misunderstandings between the artist and the client.

Both the commission of the maquette and the commission dealing with the final version should be given in contract form. In the contract involving the maquette, the responsabilities of the artist and the client should be stated, should also be included the following: the size of the maquette, its nature, the list of documents, sketches, estimate, photographs that should be provided with it, the time limits necessary for completion, the selection mode, the time limits and modalities of disclosure of the results;

*The Conseil de la Sculpture du Québec provides various forms of contracts for its members and the public.

45

should also be included the possibilities of breach of contract as well as the resultant penalties. This contract should also determine the amount of allowance as well as the conditions for authorization to reproduce the sketches or maquette, including the financial details of this use. As is true for any type of contract, a clause related to the possibility of bankruptcy by one of the contracting party should also be included, particularly with regard to the evolution of the work. This last clause should be such that the rules of ethics previously mentioned are respected, particularly those dealing with the necessity for the artist to control his creation.

The contract dealing with the commission should be even more precise. It should include a detailed description of the function of the work, the conditions necessary for its production, the mandate of the sculptor such as the theme to be used, subject matter or commemorated event, the nature of the artist's intervention, the materials, the techniques and methods used, the time limits that are set, the allowances paid by the client, their nature (lump sum or fees and reimbursement of production costs), the manner in which they will be paid as well as how the cession of the physical property rights should be carried out. Usually, a first instalment is given when the contract is signed followed by one or other subsequent instalment depending on the budget involved and the duration of the contract.

This contract should also stipulate the method used for identifying the work and the respective responsabilities of the client and the artist in this respect. Finally, the sheet describing the maintenance to be done to which is attached photographs of the work should be handed over at the same time as the work so that the best conservation measures can immediately be insured. The date and content of this maintenance specifications sheet should also be included in the contract.

If the contract deals with a limited edition of a work or works or with an edition of multiples, the precise total number should be stated as well as the conditions of the edition or reproduction. This contract must then conform with the rules of ethics previously described.

Additional clauses must be included if the commission involves a public or integrated sculpture. Obviously, the site involved is described, precisely stating the restrictions linked to the nature of the site, the environmental conditions that exist, its configuration, frequentation, circulation as well as the installation and anchoring of the sculpture. In the case of integration of sculptures, the contract should adequately inform the artist about the evolution of the architectural project and that of the building site, plan for the readjustment of budget in answer to any important change in the architecture or the work schedule which may affect the production of the art work. The contract should also define the responsabilities of the owner with regard to the exposure, maintenance, lighting and eventually the signification of the work while respecting the artist's concept. This contract also includes the duties of the artist and owner towards safety standards, civil liability and any legislation protecting the environment. These clauses also often require the use of a casualty insurance and that of any other insurance which covers the artist's death, his civil liability as well as the usual guarantee of five years against latent defects.

The needs of our society are constantly evolving thus resulting in constant modifications in the environment and frequent re-allocations of buildings and sites. In this context, it is advisable that the contracts dealing with commissioned integrated works of art include this possibility of alienation of the site and work, the possibility of its being moved while taking into account the moral right of its author and his vision concerning the evolution of his work.

Finally, the existence of a competition implies that the results be publicized as soon as possible. This constitutes an implicit agreement between the organizer and the participants. The competitors must first be informed in writing of these results. Moreover, a public disclosure of the results should also take place be it through an ad in the newspaper, a press conference or any other public event. On the other hand, the client reserves the right to disclose the results of the competition, to publicize the scale model and the sketches that were selected within the framework of an advertising campaign dealing with the project.

If the client wishes to be the first to announce the results, he should do so taking into account the copyright. These restrictions should also be defined in specific clauses in the contract for the maquette and in the commission contract.

The cost of a commission

Since the commissioned work attempts to directly satisfy the client's demands, it involves a very specific approach to artistic creation. This personal service is particularly

47

restrictive for the artist who must take into consideration, the client's expectations, his specifications and conditions for producing the work while still respecting his own professional standards towards the quality of his work and expression. The commission often requires additional research and work. This is why a commissioned work is generally much more expensive than a work resulting from the artist's pure need for expression.

When public or integrated sculptures are involved, the gap between a commissioned work and a studio work is much greater. The artist must then work with engineers or other specialists to insure that his work agrees with construction standards and rules of public safety. In fact, his code of ethics compels him to do so. In spite of these precautions, the sculptor must also pay for expensive insurance policies to protect himself against possible legal proceedings, Sometimes, he may also have to pay for the costs of installation of his work including its identification and lighting system. All these additional production costs must be included in the price therefore increasing it greatly. The sculptor must be aware of the importance of the good management of his career; this last is essential to establish a fair climate of competition with his peers as described in the code of ethics.

Photo:
Diana Boulay-Dubé setting up a temporary installation at the "Jeux d'espace" event that took place in the Old Port of Montréal in the summer of 1986. For this installation, the artist used various objects used in daily life, clothes hangers, plastic containers, colander, nylon string etc. Other installations from other participants can be seen at the back. Photograph Daniel Roussel.

Symposiums

Are symposiums a problem?

Sculptures that have been stripped, thrown in a river like so much garbage; sculptures painted over with a color different from that chosen by the author, others left to the ravages of bad weather, to the delirium of graffiti artists or even simply razed with a bulldozer; still others, moved away from the site they were designed for. Are these the results of ignorance or deliberate aggression against an "inaccessible", "elitist" art from which one feels excluded. "Affaire d'Alma", 1966-77; affaire "Corridart", 1976-81; affaire "Saint-Jean Port-Joli", 1985-89; Man and His World; Plaines d'Abraham; La Prairie. The list of the outrages to the moral rights of sculptors, acts of negligence, vandalism is long and painful. This is not restricted to Québec, far from it. Older works of art are also subjected to violence but public avant-garde sculptures remain its main target. These acts do not occur only during symposiums but are frequently seen then. The rule seems to be one of discreet silence; art maga-

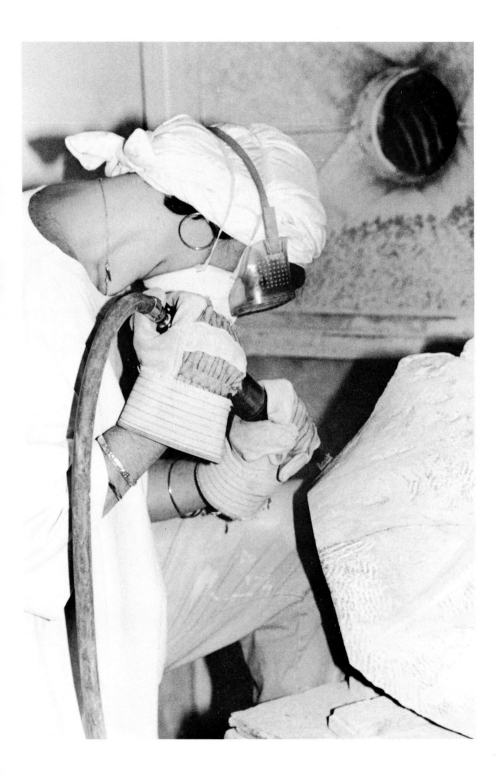

zines, American and European museums never mention these facts to avoid, so they say, any other copycat assaults and destruction.

Symposiums have also raised other problems: uneasy relationships between the artists and organizers, misunderstandings about their reciprocal responsabilities, overstepping time limits set by one or the other, breach of contract. There are very few Québécois symposiums that have not left bitter memories for the participants and organizers if only through the virulent pen of local newspaper journalists.

Nevertheless, since the Mont-Royal symposium in 1967, symposiums have been taking place regularly in Québec. This is because, despite all these mishaps, this type of event remains for the sculptor, a privileged occasion to initiate the public to their work. The symposium sometimes gives the artist a unique opportunity to produce a monumental or environmental sculpture. For municipalities, it represents a means to enrich at a small price the cultural heritage of the area. Mainly, is not the symposium, by its own definition, a lieu of communication, a sharing of experiences and knowledge? This is of course possible only if the methods used for selecting the participants do not give rise to contestation, if the roles and responsabilities of each person involved, artists, organizers, local officials are clearly defined, if the financing of the event has been guaranteed before it begins and if the local population is prepared to accept the works that are proposed. The Chicoutimi symposium, one of the few symposiums that turned out to be a real success for the participants, fulfilled all of these conditions.

The organization of a symposium
A symposium is a public event: the works are produced in front of the public, they are planned for public sites and the financing of the event is generally and largely assumed by the different levels of government. The method used for selecting the participants is therefore essential to its success. There should be no room for litigation. It is thus advisable that the methods used for choosing the participant be based on the same rules dictating the selection of artists for public commissions. It may happen that one or several artists are invited because of their expertise, relationship with the proposed theme or outstanding fame but it is preferable to proceed with a public competition and jury. The previous chapter deals with the selection itself.

Photo:
Female sculptor directly carving with a pneumatic chisel. The artist has rigorously respected health and safety standards, protecting herself adequately. Photograph Martin Brault

The choice and exploitation of the theme which frequently comes down to the common use of a technique or material are also important. This sharing of a common approach to sculpture is more than just a pretext; it stimulates intellectual and professional exchanges between the participants and intensifies the interaction that occurs between the works. This must facilitate communication between artists and public and the harmonious insertion of the works in the sites for which they were constructed. On the other hand, the theme must be open to large and flexible interpretation so that the artist's freedom of expression is not restricted. This requires from the organizer a degree of openness and sustained public relations efforts around this common point of interest, both before and during the event. Several of the previously stated problems could have been avoided if, to begin with, the organizers had better defined their objectives. Should the symposium be used for popular education? How important should the intellectual and professional exchanges be between the participants? Should these exchanges take place at meetings, conferences? If so,should these talks and discussions be more widely open to other artists and other art experts? Should the public be admitted to these specialized communications?

The choice of the location and works is also of prime importance and this even more so now since artists have become interested in the integration of their work to the environment. In a symposium, the site has even more importance in the elaboration of the work. Since the symposium is a specific event, even an historic one, the interrelationships between the work and the geo-physical and socio-cultural characteristics of the site are more evident. Furthermore, when several works of the symposium are produced on the same site, there necessarily occurs formal exchanges between them, a type of symbiosis which makes them almost indissociable from each other. If the works completed in this context were to be moved, the entire site would also have to be moved so that the works would not be altered. The organizers should therefore choose a site that is permanent and which will not be alienated. If this is impossible, it is necessary to warn the participants of this when they are invited and when the contract is signed and also plan for the removal of the works as well as the methods and conditions necessary to change the location.

A symposium can also be designed as a short-lived

exhibit-event of ephemeral work that will be destroyed or given back to the artist once the event is over. The risks of controversy are much lessened if the organizers inform the artists of their intentions with respect to the permanent or short-lived character of the site and the works as soon as the invitation to participate is made. The artist's participation constitutes an acceptation of these conditions. The fact that the transfer of the works had already been planned in the Chicoutimi symposium contract has probably contributed to the success of the event for the participants. On the other hand, the lack of precision of the contract of the Saint-Jean-Port-Joli symposium with regard to how the eventual transfer of the titles of property of the site and the works would be carried out has allowed the new owner of the site to destroy one sculpture and contributed to the inappropriate location of the others, generally resulting in the artists's dissatisfaction.

To these questions, one must also add that of the allotment of the sites. It may seem to be desirable that these sites be alloted before the event begins. However, If no major problem is involved and if no additional costs of lay-out, services or transport of materials are incurred, the organizers should be rather flexible and permit the exchange of sites between participants.

Sculpture symposiums usually last a few weeks or months. This is rather a short time if a large dimension work is to be produced. To avoid any ambiguity which would result in undue delays, it is essential that the responsibilities of the organizers and artist be clearly established both when the invitation is made and in the contract. Who will be the owner of the works and what will be his responsibilities with regard to their conservation? How will the participants be transported and where will they live? Who will pay for this? What remuneration will the artist receive and how will the payments be made? In what way will the materials and technical services be furnished? What will be the limits of the responsibility and budget of the organizers in this area? Will third parties, firms or public services be associated to the prestation of materials or services? If this is the case, the organizers will have to be the intermediary between the agencies and patrons on one hand and the artists on the other hand. They will have to make sure that the materials and services are provided in time so the artists can honor their contract and time limits. Should the artist plan for all his needs in the technical specifications form that he hands over with the maquette? Or will he be able to increase his demands while producing the work if the context in which he executes the work is modified? What will be the maximum budget allowed for production costs? In a symposium, the working site is usually open to the public, which does increase the risk of accidents. Who will be responsible for these risks and the civil liabilities on the working site: the artist, the organizer or the municipality? To what amount should the responsible agent be insured? Who will be responsible for the civil liabilities once the work is completed and for how long? What will be the time limits for the various tasks and execution of the work? To what degree should the artist be present on the site? How strictly will he have to stick to a precise schedule? What will happen if these agreements are not respected by one or the other party involved? Will penalties be incurred?

Copies of contracts designed for just this type of event can be found at the offices of the Conseil de la Sculpture du Québec.

The symposium, a communication event

The definition of the word symposium implies a place where communication can take place. Thus, exchanges are an integral part of the duties of the participants and the responsabilities of the organizers. The symposium is before anything else a place where exchanges between experts occur. In a sculpture symposium, these exchanges can be formalized in public talks, panel discussions, even a collaboration to a collective work. But the richness of a symposium resides more in the daily exchanges of services, technical informations, professional experiences, knowledge and thoughts about art. The role of the artist is then to be as open as possible to these exchanges, to be at the same time available and curious towards the other participants. The organizers should facilitate these interactions through their attentive presence and through the organization of informal meetings and general activities.

Symposiums sometimes make it possible for participants to step out of their established fields. This is true for most sculpture symposiums where sculptors often have to be confronted with other experts from various fields such as philosophers, critics, art historians and others that are concerned with the arts. The organization of tours guided by critics and curators of public and pri-

54

vate collections, or still informal meetings between the participants and other art experts or even with other experts concerned with the theme of the symposium can further facilitate these wider exchanges.

We have previously emphasized the importance of communication with the public, with its artistic training. This communication must take place much before the opening of the symposium; this is particularly important if the works that will be produced are quite different from the idea of art the public entertains. It is necessary to create some complicity with this public so that it may feel that it participates in the event and may be proud of it.

Here, the medias play a major role. This is particularly true for the local medias, closer to the public and mainly for television which has now become for the working-class an authority, a tool for social consecration. Some promotional means have been successfully used by the organizers of symposiums, namely, the exhibition of the selected maquettes, their publications in a leaflet or catalog, their diffusion in local media even an invitation to the public to participate in the selection. Cultural activities including the participation of the artists or other specialists could also result in a better understanding of the works and thus their acceptance by the public. For instance, the following can be used: guided tours, game-competitions involving the works, beginner sculpture workshops for the children or even families and even the creation by the public of a collective work of art. Ultimately, an attempt should be made to create around these symposium works a sense of belonging linked to the sense of being a member of the community itself. This powerful link between the community and the works would best protect these against vandalism and destruction.

The evolution of the works and site

Once the symposium is over and if the organizers have selected a permanent site, they should make sure through a contract that the owner of the site will honour his commitments with regard to the identification of the works, respect their integration to the site, the maintenance of the site and works in accordance with the maintenance estimate form supplied by the artists. If a temporary site was chosen, they must make sure that the works will either be removed by the artists within a specific time if these are the owners or removed with all necessary precautions to a permanent site.

55

CHAPTER 4

Explicative notes about copyright in Canada

The Canadian copyright law which has been modified in 1988, establishes the rights of the authors of artistic works such as sculptures. However, to be protected, the work must be original, that is, not been copied from somebody else's work. The law also accepts that the sculpture work includes molds and models.

Copyright exists automatically, it requires no **registration**. Such a registration is however possible and makes it easier to prove the existence of the copyright at a given period in time.

The author of the work is the first holder of the copyright attached to it. Generally, the duration of copyright includes the lifetime of the artist and a period of fifty years after his death.

The copyright is made up of bodies of distinct rights with which the author can compromise separately, that is, he can cede some of these rights to another party. Among others, these rights include the exclusive right to produce and reproduce the work and the right to present an artistic work to the public. The right also includes the exclusive right to authorize the acts previously mentioned.

Since 1988, the moral rights of the author have been added to the pecuniary rights; these moral rights have the same duration and conditions appended.

These rights include the right to claim the creation of a work (or to remain anonymous), the right to make sure the integrity of the work is respected and finally the right of endorsement which allows the author to control any association of his work with a product, cause or agency by forbidding such an association if it is detrimental to his honor or reputation.

While the author can cede one or the other of the author's rights, the moral rights cannot be ceded. The his may however renounce them in part or completely. When the author dies, the authors' rights that he has not ceded to third parties are passed on to his heirs or legatees as are his moral rights on his works.

The law obviously makes provision for appeals which the author may use against those that would infringe upon his copyright or his moral rights. These appeals are civil in nature, that is, they allow the author for instance to ask for an injunction, damages for violation of copyright, an accounting for profits made by the copyright infringer and a restitution of funds that were received illegally by the person violating the law. The law also makes provision for penal appeals sanctionned by fines and even imprisonment.

To insure that in Canada the rights of foreign artists are also respected and those of Canadian artists respected outside this country, Canada has committed itself to international conventions and protocols which mainly have for effect the creation of a reciprocity system.

Those who buy works of art should know that acquisition of a work of art does not include the acquisition of the copyright on it. In effect, unless otherwise stated, the right to reproduce the work or to publish photographs of it remains the exclusive property of the artist. Furthermore the property rights are in a way restricted by the moral rights of the author. The buyer cannot distort, mutilate or otherwise modify the work of art unless the author has authorized such behavior. The moral rights of the author therefore commit the buyer to protecting the work against any distortion, mutilation or other modification.

In conclusion, the copyright and the moral rights deal with the work as means of for expression. The alienation of one of the elements of the copyright does not bring about the alienation of the other pecuniary rights so that the author decides, every time he cedes a right, to what degree he lets go of his work. This also holds true for moral rights, since these can be renounced in part or totally. Whether one is a user, buyer or author of a work of art, it is important to know that there exist several components to copyright which together define and delineate the intellectual property of the work.

Conclusion

Before proceeding with a purchase, a commission or even the organization of a sculpture event, the consumers or their representatives should be well aware of the nature and extent of the agreements involved and they should also assess correctly the importance of the materials and services with which they must provide the participants. They also must clearly state their expectations. In sum, they must clearly stipulate the artists's responsibilities, their own responsibilities and assume these completely.

For their part, the artists must be honest and careful in all their business dealings. They must study closely the proposed conditions and if necessary negotiate them. Once these conditions have been accepted, they must scrupulously respect their verbal and written agreements. This is essential to establish harmonious relation-

57

ships with their financial and social partners, clients, backers, organizers of events or media people. The quality of these relationships remains one of the best means to promote their profession and their art.

Photo:
Yves Trudeau arc welding (electrical welding) the various components of an assembled sculpture. The components of an assembled sculpture are usually joined together by welding or bolting. Photograph Luc Chartier.

Lexicon

Alloy: metallic product obtained from the combination or mixing of various metals and/or metaloids while these are in a liquid state. More widely, the term is used to describe mixtures of non-metallic materials, for instance wax or plastic alloys.

Art bronze: 1. Alloy containing more than 65% copper **2.** Work of art produced with this alloy.

Artistic concept: mental representation of the art object as projected by the artist.

Artist's proof: copies intended for the artist and his collaborators and produced on top of the copies of the prescribed edition or intended for sale. Each artist's proof is labelled AP followed by the identification number in Roman numbers, the numerator being the number of the artist's proof and the denominator the size of the edition of artist's proof. Those copies which are used only as samples and which are not for sale are labelled hors commerce.

Art object: authentic, unique work or one which is part of a limited edition and which is then numbered.

Assembling: 1. Sculpture produced by combining various elements that once linked together constitute a whole, a single work of art. This assembling may require the use of several techniques: stapling, bolting, riveting, screwing, gluing, embedding, welding, brazing, forging, etc. **2.** Operation used to assemble the various elements of a complex work that were cast separately.

Bronze: alloy of copper and pewter to which is eventually added other elements such as zinc and lead; each of these additions affects its look and other physical properties.

Bust: sculpture representing the upper part of a human body, that is, the head and torso, either in totality or in part.

Carving: subtraction sculpture process through which the sculpture is produced using a material from which some elements are removed with the help of chisels, gouges, or other sharp cutting, manual or electrical tools. Carving is often used for making wood, stone, ceramics, ice or snow sculptures.

Photo: "Dérouler, dérouler", performance by Robert Racine at the Montréal Contemporary Art Museum in 1979. Here, the artist combines theatre with an installation sculpture. Photograph Robert Etcheverry.

61

Cast: 1. Set of techniques linked to the production of a copy in melted metal or alloy. Casting includes the production of a mold from the model, prototype or its reproduction, the fusion of the material, the casting, the unmolding, repairing and if necessary finishing. **2.** Iron and carbon alloy sometimes used in sculpture.

Casting: 1. Operation which consists in melting a metal, an alloy or other material and placing it in a mold while it is still in a liquid or pasty state. **2.** The result from this operation.

Conservation: combination of methods and techniques used for maintaining the original aspect of a work. Some of these are used to prevent the deterioration of the object while others have to do with restoration, an attempt to return to its original state an object that has deteriorated. *(pp 26, 28, 29, 46, 53)*

Copy: reproduction of an original work of art; each of the art objects reproducing a common work having an edition limited to twelve or less. There is a difference between the copies from a limited edition and the copies from a multiple. Each copy in the edition is identified with a fraction, the numerator indicating the specific number of the copy and the denominator the total size of the edition. Arab numbers are used for the edition produced for marketing. This identification is usually inscribed at the bottom or even under the base of the work. *(pp 7, 9, 12, 15 to 18, 20, 22, 29, 47, 51)*

Corrosion: modifications, often superficial of the physical properties (color, texture) of an alloy or metal, caused by natural or artificial chemical actions.

Edition: 1. Casting or assembling techniques used for reproducing copies of the same prototype, model or mold. **2.** Set of copies produced by this method. **3.** Total number of copies. Contrary to the situation found in the field of engraving where the artist must adhere to the rule of uniformity of the copies within the same edition, including uniformity in form, drawing, texture, relief, and color, in the field of sculpture, variations of color, materials, patina, heightening between copies of the same edition are acceptable as long as the form remains unaltered. Thus, part of the edition can be produced in bronze, another in aluminum, silver or any other material. Furthermore, the patina or heightenings can be different from copy to copy.

Edition: 1. The set of copies of an original sculpture made from the same model, prototype or mold. **2.** In locution, "edition bronze" referring to a multiple of a work produced in an unlimited number, is used in the sense of reproduction. This expression, long used in Europe, is today replaced by "multiple" which is less confusing. *(pp 6, 7, 9, 10, 11, 12, 15 to 22, 25, 26 30, 44, 45, 46)*

Edition bronze: widely diffused bronze sculpture; not numbered. edition bronzes are considered to be multiples and not original work of art. The term "multiple" is used most frequently.

Engraver: in Québec, indicates any artist working in the field of engraving, that is, who creates and produces works of art by using matrices which will be printed using one or the other printing technique. It includes those who use aquatint, etching, lithography and silk-screening. The engraver should not be confused with the master printer who simply executes the work.

Enlargment: transfer of an art work to a scale greater than that originally planned for it. Reproduction resulting from this operation.

Environmental: is said about a sculpture that uses among its components, or as a main component, the environment surrounding its site or one of these elements: earth, stone, air, water, snow, wind, constructions.

Finish: textures, patinas of surface materials which complete the production of a sculpture giving it its definitive look. This finish is sometimes protected with a varnish or wax.

Finishing: set of operations which result in the improvement and the completion of the exterior aspect of a sculpture. These finishing techniques include polishing, burnishing, veneering, natural or artificial patinas, painting.

Gallery owner: in Québec, an art dealer which combines dealership with a purely cultural work of art diffusion and the promotion of artists he represents. The gallery owner is essentially interested in the marketing of living artists.

Heightening: 1. Touches or strokes of acid or paint applied on the surface of a sculpture aimed at increasing its volume, relief, texture or the effects of light on the work. **2.** Operation used for modifiyng a sculpture or an engraving.

Hologram: original photographic image producing images that have relief and color thanks to the interferences of the beams of laser rays. The hologram is an image that is not material and which appears to be suspended in the air. When used by artists this technique allows the reproduction of artistic works.

Hors commerce: sample copy exclusively used for documentation, advertising, marketing and which should never be sold. These copies should be identified with the letters HC. *(pp 7, 17)*

Imitation bronze: melted zinc covered with a metallic coating imitating the patina of bronze.

Insertion: introduction of a work of art in a site for which it had not been planned when first created.

Installation: sculptural work generally made up of several dispersed elements in a given space and having a theatrical character. The installation may use natural elements, found objects that are transformed or not and/or objects created by the artist.

Integration: conception and installation of a sculpture produced in relation to the main characteristics of the site to which it is destined. Through integration, the artist attempts to incorporate in the work some elements of the site in such a way the work of art and the site become interdependant.

Limited Edition sculpture: sculpture produced in a limited pre-determined number of copies. *(pp 11, 12, 15, 17, 18, 19)*

Maquette: rough model or complete model of a sculpture.

Mold: solid body, hollow or shaped, flexible or hard in which is poured a liquid or paste that becomes solid through drying and/or cooling and which keeps the shape determined by this matrix. In the field of art bronzes, a difference is made between on one hand the molds which can be reused, molds that are not hollow, which are etched and/or produced through later assembling and the flexible molds which during casting, must be supported with a rigid plaster or stratified resin shell and on the other hand the lost wax molds which can be used to produce only one copy since they must be destroyed to recover the sculpture.

Molding: 1. process used for making objects or sculptures starting from molds. **2.** Art object made from a mold.

Monument: sculpture used for commemorating an event.

Monumental: is said about an art work whose large size is similar to that of an architectural work.

Multiple: reproduction of a work of art in an unlimited number of copies. *(pp 17 to 20, 46)*

Original work of art: unique work or work belonging to a prescribed limited edition each copy of which is numbered including the artist's proof copies and the hors commerce copies.

Overmolding: reproduction using plaster, metallic alloy, resin, hard rubber or any other material produced from a molding and not from the original model or prototype.

Patina: Transformation of the surface of a sculpture giving it its definitive aspect. Patinas can be created naturally due to the effects of weather or artificially with the use of various acids applied on the surface of the work. Metals, wood, plaster can acquire a patina. The patina of bronzes is often accelerated by the use of acids. The acid patinas obtained through an acidification process, do not blister or disintegrate since they become an integral part of the metal. An aspect of patina can also be obtained with the application of colored waxes or paints that only partially penetrate into the material. These patinas are used for metals, wood and plasters. This type of patina can eventually disintegrate. On the other hand, it is less sensitive than a natural or acid patina to stains and is more easily cleaned up if an accident occurs. There are no two identical patinas. Minimal differences in the chemical content, density and solution of the acid, the temperature when applied, the surface texture can result in very different effects. The patina is part of the work; one should never apply something on a sculpture which may alter its patina.

Performance: in visual arts, a work of art whose duration and methods for production are an integral part of the work; its theatrical character and the use of the time factor links it with the entertainment arts. Visual arts performances sometimes use elements that are generally used in entertainment arts such as movement, sound, musique, acting, choreography and scenography. Performances are usually ephemeral works.

Performance sculpture: sculpture work that is generally transient in nature, is shown in public; the process used for producing the work and the time factor are both important elements of this type of work.

Posthumous work: copy of a work produced from a prototype, model, scale model or mold after the death of the artist and on which the artist could not exert an absolute control.

Prototype: concerns original works of art produced by casting techniques, first model or reference model which is used for making the flexible mold from which another plaster mold or several wax copies in the case of lost wax molding. The prototype is also called pre-model. For sculptures that are assembled, it is the first copy of a model which is then used for producing the copies of an edition. *(pp 6, 7, 9, 10, 12, 15, 16, 36)*

Public art: work of art, either privately or publicly owned and placed on a site that is accessible at all times.

Reduction: transfer of a work of art in a smaller size than originally planned when first conceived. Reproduction resulting from this operation.

Registration: inscription in a public register of the intellectual property rights on a creation by the author or one eligible party. In Canada, registration is not mandatory for an original work of art. The Copyright Registration Office is responsible for this task.

Relief: a mural made up of tridimensional elements that are more or less separated from the background. There are various types of reliefs: bas-relief showing slight protrusions from plain background, haut-reliefs showing more obvious protrusions from the background and ronde-bosse whose relief is so removed from the background that it becomes possible to partially circumvent the work.

Scale: 1. Relationship to an order of dimension... **2.** In sculpture, the relationship of an enlargement, reduction or maquette to the final version of work.

Sculpture: tridimensional object or relief designed by an artist which is defined by its author as a work of art. This is a very wide definition which includes as sculptures, reliefs, assemblings, installations, conversion of spaces or territories linking it to environmental art or performance and other contemporary forms of this art.

Seal: official mark of an artist, workshop or editor whose print is applied on or under the base of a sculpture to authenticate it. The seal can be affixed directly in the paste before it becomes solid or can be placed on a piece of metal similar to a coin which is then fixed to the base of the work when finishing takes place. In this last case, the caster plans for a small cavity in which this piece is attached once the work is completed. In sculpture, the artist's seal often replaces his signature.

Site: configuration of a place, piece of land or building where a sculpture is installed.

Size of the edition: total number of copies of an edition of a work of art.

State: 1. Various aspects of an etching plate before it is completed. **2.** Edition which corresponds to the printing of each of these stages of the plate. **3.** By association, this term could be extended to sculpture to distinguish between the variations in finish, texture, patina, heightening of the surface or still the variations in materials from one copy to the other when all the copies of an original edition are not absolutely identical. **(p. 19)**

Statue: sculpture showing a complete standing human being.

Symposium: 1. Work seminar that brings together a limited number of artists with varying backgrounds around a common theme, material or technique with the aim of producing one or several sculptures on a common site or sites close to each other and to facilitate intellectual and professional exchanges between these participants. **2.** Set of sculptures produced at such an event.

TECHNICAL SPECIFICATIONS FORM

Name of the artist. . . . .
Title of the work. . . . .
Copy number. . . . .
Date of creation of prototype. . . . .
Date of casting or assembling. . . . .
Caster or practitioner. . . . .
Place of production. . . . .
Editor. . . . .

GENERAL CHARACTERISTICS
Material(s). . . . .
Technique(s) and production method(s). . . . .
Number of elements: assembled ❏ . . . . non-assembled ❏ . . . .
Assembling: method(s) and technique(s). . . . .
Localization of assembly joints. . . . .
Inside: full ❏   hollow ❏   inner wall aspect(s). . . . .
Surface aspects (finish, coating, decor, color(s), technique(s) and
material(s) used). . . . .
Dimensions: height. . . . . width. . . . . depth. . . . .
Thickness of material. . . . .

Description of the base or support:
Form. . . . .
Material(s). . . . .
Anchor system. . . . .
Dimensions: height. . . . . width. . . . . depth. . . . .

COPIES OF THE EDITION *(if relevant)*
Edition number. . . . . Artist's proof. . . . . Hors commerce. . . . .
Seal ❏ or signature of the author ❏ technique. . . . . . . location. . . . .
Seal of caster ❏   technique. . . . . . . location. . . . .
Seal of workshop ❏   technique. . . . . . . location. . . . .
Seal of editor ❏   technique. . . . . . . location. . . . .
Other(s) inscription(s) ❏   technique. . . . . . . location. . . . .
Reduction(s) or enlargement(s) ❏ . . . .
Scale(s) and size of the edition. . . . .

CONSERVATION, INSTALLATION
Permanent work ❏   Ephemeral work ❏
Mobile work ❏   Integration work ❏

Location	Date	Artist's signature

LIGHTING, INSTALLATION AND MAINTENANCE SPECIFICATIONS

IDENTIFICATION OF THE WORK
Name of artist. . . . .
Title of the work. . . . .
Copy number. . . . .
Date of creation of prototype. . . . .
Date of casting or assembling. . . . .
Caster or practitioner. . . . .

Materials   Trademark   Address of supplier
. . . .
. . . .
. . . .

Dimensions:
    assembled: height. . . . . . .   width. . . . .   depth . . . .
    not-assembled: height. . . . . . .   width. . . . .   depth . . . .
Total weight. . . . . Weight of main components. . . . .

Location
ground ❑   wall ❑   ceiling ❑   others ❑ (describe). . . . .
accessible to public ❑   limited access ❑   inaccessible to the public ❑
Installation methods. . . . .
Clearance space if desired. . . . .
Support ❑   pedestal ❑   anchor ❑   others ❑ (describe). . . . .
Lay-out (water, electricity,). . . . . etc. (Include a plan). . . . .
. . . .
Site of exhibition :   indoor ❑   outdoor ❑
Natural aging: desired ❑   not desired ❑
Maintenance   yes ❑   no ❑
Polishing   yes ❑   no ❑
Cleaning   yes ❑   no ❑
Refinishing   yes ❑   no ❑
Removal of graffitis yes ❑   no ❑
Other(s). . . . .
The frequency and methods to be used for maintenance can be found in the annex; the services of specialists may sometimes be necessary.
Handling and transport (vulnerability of the work, packing specifications and necessary precautions). . . . .

  Location   Date   Artist's signature

                                  Client's signature

BIBLIOGRAPHY

BERMAN, Harold, Bronze Sculptors: 1800-1930, Abage Publishers, Chicago, 1974. CRUIKSHANK, Jeffrey and KORZA, Pam, Going Public: A Field Guide to Developments in Arts in Public Places, published by the Art Services Extension of University of Massachusetts in collaboration with the Visual Arts program of the National Endowment for the Arts, Amherst, 1988. DORNBERG, John, "Arts Vandals: Why do they do it?", Art News, New York, March 1987. DUMAS, Roland, La propriété littéraire et artistique, Éditions Thémis, Presses universitaires de France, Paris, 1987. GIBSON, Eric, "Public Art and the Public Realm", Sculpture, Washington, january-february, 1988. GRANT, Daniel, "The Unknown Soldiers of the Art World", American Artists, December, 1987. HOCHFIELD, Sylvia, "Casting Doubt", Art News, New York, february, 1989. MORRIS, Kenneth, "Rethinking Sculpture Conservation", Sculpture, Washington, November-December 1987. PERKIN, Jeanne, Art in Architecture: Art fort the Built Environnement in the Province of Ontario, published by Visual Arts Ontario, Toronto, 1982. ROMA, Jean-Pierre, Le bronze d'art et ses techniques, Éditions H. VIAL, Paris, 1988. THALACKER, Donald, The Place of Art in the World of Architecture, Chelsea House Publishers in collaboration with R. R. Bowker Company, New York, London, 1980. TRUSTMAN, Deborah, "Abuses in the Reproduction of Sculpture", Art News, Summer, New York, 1981. « CODE DE DÉONTOLOGIE ET GUIDE PRATIQUE À L'INTENTION DES PERSONNES ŒUVRANT DANS LE DOMAINE DE LA CONSERVATION », 2e édition. Institut international pour la conservation. Groupe canadien. Association des restaurateurs professionnels. Ottawa, 1989. COLLEGE ART ASSOCIATION, "A statement on Standards for Sculpture: Reproduction and Preventive Measures to Combat Unethical Casting in Bronze", Washington, April 24, 1974. MINISTERE DES AFFAIRES CULTURELLES, La sauvegarde des monuments de bronze, Publications du Québec, Québec, 1988. MINISTERE DES AFFAIRES CULTURELLES, Loi 78: Loi sur le Statut professionnel des artistes des arts visuels, des métiers d'art et de la littérature et sur leurs contrats avec les diffuseurs, Éditeur officiel du Québec, Québec, 1988. MINISTERE DE LA CULTURE ET DE LA COMMUNICATION, Inventaire général des monuments et richesses artistiques de France, La sculpture: méthode et vocabulaire. Principes d'analyse scientifique, Imprimerie nationale, Paris, 1980. MINISTERE DES COMMUNICATIONS, Law C-60: Law modifying the Copyright Law, Ottawa, 1988.

USEFUL ADDRESSES:

Association des restaurateurs professionnels
Boîte postale 9195
Ottawa, Ontario
K1G 3T9.

CSQ (Conseil de la sculpture du Québec)
911, rue Jean-Talon est
Montréal (Québec)
H2R 1V5.
(514) 270-7209

SODAAV (Société des droits d'auteur en arts visuels)
1229 rue Panet
Montréal (Québec)
H2L 2Y6.
(514) 525-5201

SERVICES OFFERED BY THE CONSEIL DE LA SCULPTURE DU QUÉBEC:

Consultation of slide bank of members'works for groups wishing to acquire sculptures. Display shelf holding the complete dossiers of our members available at the office of the CSQ.

Lighted display shelf of slides showing our members's works; available at the offices of the CSQ and at the Montreal Contemporary Art Museum.

Documentation center offering, books, catalogs and magazines dealing with the field of sculpture. Sculpture renting program: our members'sculptures are being rented to firms.

Professional expert services dealing with sculpture.

ACKNOWLEDGEMENTS

We wish to thank the following members of the commitee who have prepared this code of ethics and make sure it was published: Jacques Besner, Ninon Gauthier, Denise Lapointe, Luc LaRochelle, Jules Lasalle and Sylvie Rochette.

We are also grateful to every sculptor, members or not of the Conseil de la Sculpture, who has given us informations concerning their practices, experiences with the relationships they had with the buyers, users and distributors of their works, their needs in term of informations about professional ethics. We particularly want to express our appreciation to the art historians, François-Marc Gagnon and Lise Lamarche as well as the art critic, Gaston Saint-Pierre who have helped us define sculpture in the context of the writing of a code of ethics; we also appreciate the contribution of the gallery owners we consulted with, the Artcast Inc. Foundry, Me Sylviane Maurier, lawyer, Bruno Gagnon and Ghyslain Roussel, Direction des arts et lettres à l'architecture et à l'environnement and the staff of the Centre de Conservation du Québec, these last three attached to the Ministère des Affaires culturelles du Québec. We could not have carried out this work without their help.

This work has been published with the financial support of the Ministère des Affaires culturelles du Québec and The Samuel & Saidye Bronfman Family Foundation and thanks to the provision of services and donations from Pratt & Whitney Canada and The Reader's Digest Association (Canada) Ltd, to which we express our heartfelt gratitude.

CONSEIL DE LA SCULPTURE DU QUÉBEC